Introduction to Syriac Reading and Writing

Gorgias Handbooks

23

Series Editor

George Anton Kiraz

The Gorgias Handbooks series provides students and scholars with textbooks and reference books useful for the classroom and for research.

Introduction to Syriac Reading and Writing

George A. Kiraz

gorgias press
2011

Gorgias Press LLC, 954 River Road, Piscataway, NJ, 08854, USA

www.gorgiaspress.com

Copyright © 2011 by Gorgias Press LLC

2011   ܝ

ISBN 978-1-4632-0085-5   ISSN 1935-6838

Printed in the United States of America

Preface

This book constitutes Chapter 1 of *The New Syriac Primer* (Gorgias Press, 2007). The purpose of this extract is to make available to summer camps, community educational programs, and other non-academic classroom settings a textbook for teenagers and adult students. Having said that, academic students may use this chapter as a preparatory text before attending classes at the university level, especially if they have no training in any other Semitic language. Those who wish to continue with this method of teaching may obtain a copy of *The New Syriac Primer* which explains the basics of Syriac grammar as well.

The chapter is divided into 9 lessons. Most lessons introduce three or four letters of the alphabet at a time, with review lessons interspersed. By the end, the student is expected to be able to read vocalized and partially vocalized texts, write words and sentences, understand more than 70 words, and understand basic sentences.

All the reading sections can be downloaded in audio format from the Gorgias Press web site by search for the page of *The New Syriac Primer*.

July 15, 2011
Feast of Mor Quryaqos and his mother Yuliti.

George Anton Kiraz

1   Olaph, Béth, Gomal, and Dolath

The Letters

Each letter of the Syriac alphabet has a name. The first four letters are listed below:

Name	Syriac	Hebrew	Arabic	Sound
Olaph	ܐ	א	ا	(silent)
Béth	ܒ	ב	ب	b
Gomal	ܓ	ג	Egyptian ج	g
Dolath	ܕ	ד	د	d

The first column, labeled 'Name', gives the name of each of the four letters. The second column, labeled 'Syriac', gives the shapes of the letters in the Serto script (there are two other scripts, Estrangelo and East Syriac, which we will cover in Chapter 8). The next two columns give the Hebrew and Arabic equivalents in case you know either language (if you do not, simply ignore them). The last column gives the sound of the letters. This table structure will be followed in subsequent sections of this chapter.

Béth is pronounced as *b* in *boy*, Gomal as *g* in *give*, and Dolath as *d* in *Dad*. In West Syriac pronunciation, Olaph is silent in most contexts, especially in words introduced in this chapter.

Syriac is written from right to left. When letters are combined to form words, they are connected to each other, like English handwriting. For example, the sequence Gomal Béth is written as follows:

ܓܒ

Some letters connect to other letters *only* on the right. Olaph and Dolath are such letters. For example, in the sequence Béth Olaph Béth, the letter Olaph connects only to the preceding Béth (i.e., the Béth on its right):

ܒܐܒ

Note also that in this context, Olaph takes a more straight shape. Compare Olaph when it is at the beginning of the word (with a curvy shape ܐ), and when it is connected to another letter (with a straight shape ܠ) in the sequence Olaph Béth Olaph:

ܐܒܐ

Similarly, Dolath connects only to letters on its right as shown in the sequence Olaph Béth Dolath:

اِّحب

Note that the shape of ، changes to ، when it connects to other letters.

The following table summarizes how letters connect to each other.

	Final Position	Middle Position	Initial Position	Stand-alone Position
Olaph	ܠܐ	ܟܐܟ	ܟܐ	ܐ
Béth	ܒ	ܒܒܒ	ܒ	ܒ
Gomal	ܓ	ܓܓ	ܓ	ܓ
Dolath	ܒ	ܒܒ	ܘܒ	،

The 'Final Position' column gives the shapes of letters at the end of words, the 'Middle Position' column gives the shapes of letters in the middle of words, etc.

Some Vowels

Try reading aloud the following sequences.

"How can I read sequences of letters if there are no vowels in between?" you say. Exactly!

Unlike English, Syriac vowels are not written on the same line as letters. They are written above the letters (some times below, but I will not inflict that upon you). Imagine the English word *boy*, being written with the vowel *o* on top of the *b* as follows:

o
by

Here are three Syriac vowels, the shape of each is shown above a dotted circle, ○. The doted circle represents the letter on which the vowel is written.

Name	Shape	Sound
Phthoḥo	○	Read *a* as in *man*
Zqopho	○	Read *o* as in *go*
Rboṣo	○	Read *e* as in *men*

Each vowel has a name which you don't have to memorize, but you can impress people if you do! (Don't worry about the dots under 'h' in Phthoḥo and 's' in Rboṣo for now.)

You can get the exact pronunciation of the vowels when we read the text below. Basically, placing ó over the letter ܒ gives ܒ̇, which is read *ba*. Similarly, placing ó over ܓ gives ܓ̇, read *go*, and placing ó over ܕ gives ܕ̇, read *dé*.

Reading for the Very First Time
Read the following with the help of the CD. For now, I will be giving you the transliteration. But start getting used to reading without transliterations as I will no longer give them in later sections. It's a tough world out there!

ܐ̰	ܐ̇	ܐ̰	1
é	o	a	
ܒ̰	ܒ̇	ܒ̰	2
bé	bo	ba	
ܓ̰	ܓ̇	ܓ̰	3
gé	go	ga	
ܕ̰	ܕ̇	ܕ̰	4
dé	do	da	

English	Read	Syriac Word	
father	a-bo	ܐܰܒܳܐ	5
baby	bo-bo	ܒܳܒܳܐ	6
fruit	é-bo	ܐܶܒܳܐ	7
uncle	do-do	ܕܳܕܳܐ	8
side	ga-bo	ܓܰܒܳܐ	9
bear	dé-bo	ܕܶܒܳܐ	10
was lost	é-bad	ܐܶܒܰܕ	11
Baghdad	bag-dad	ܒܰܓܕܰܕ	12
elected, chose	gbo	ܓܒܳܐ	13

Read the above repeatedly until you are comfortable that you mastered each word before moving on.

Notes

1. Did you notice that ܵ and ܵ sound the same? Similarly, ܠ and ܠ, and ; and ܐ; have the same pronunciation, respectively. In other words, ܐ is silent at the end of words. This is also the case when other vowels are used as shown in the following example pairs:

$$ ܠ = ܵ \qquad ܐ; = ; \qquad ܠ = ܠ $$
$$ ܠ = ܵ \qquad ܐ; = ; \qquad ܠ = ܠ $$

2. Did you notice that some words have the same letters but differ in vowels? Make sure you do not confuse them. Here are two pairs as an example:

ܐܒܐ   *father*   ܐܒܐ   *fruit*

ܓܒܐ   *side*   ܓܒܐ   *elected*

3. You may find it difficult at the beginning to pronounce two letters when they come next to each other without an intervening vowel such as ܒ in ܓܒܐ. This can be mastered only by practice and repetition.

Phrases

It is hard to come up with phrases or sentences with the few words we covered, but let us try nevertheless. For each sentence, I will give the literal translation of each word directly under it, then give a more idiomatic English translation in *italic*.

ܐܒܐ   ܓܒܐ   ܐܒܐ   1
uncle   elected   father

The father elected the uncle.

ܐܒܐ   ܓܒܐ   ܐܒܐ   2
father   elected   uncle

The uncle elected the father.

ܐܒܕ   ܕܒܐ   3
was lost   bear

The bear was lost.

Writing Syriac for the Very First Time

Remember that Syriac is written from right to left. The following images guide you to writing the letters we just learned. These were done by a calligrapher[1] and differ a bit from the font used in the book. The numbers indicate the beginning of a stroke.

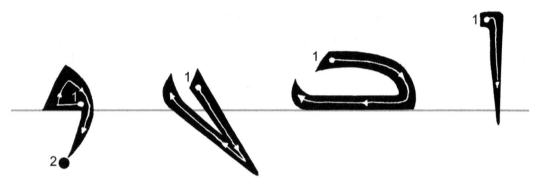

The letter ܐ is written from the top to the bottom with one stroke. The calligrapher in this case used a straight ܐ, but you can curve it a bit if you like. Note that the bottom of ܐ goes a bit below the writing line.

The letter ܒ is also written in one stroke. The letter sits on the writing line.

The letter ܓ is also written in one stroke. About one third of the letter is above the writing line. The calligrapher in this case writes ܓ in a sharper angle than the printed version shown in this book. It is up to you to use the angle you want. I usually write it closer to the printed version.

The letter ܕ is written in two strokes, but the arrow of the first stroke requires an explanation. In the first stroke, the pen starts from the white circle at point 1 and moves clockwise. When the pen reaches the white circle where you began, you start filling the top part clockwise with each circle moving closer to the center until the entire thing is filled. Then you move the pen to a position where you can begin writing the tail under the writing line, all of this in one stroke. When you fill in the top part, you basically go in a clockwise motion from the outside of the letter to the inside, and then move again to the outside to get to the point where you draw the tail. The second stroke is simply a dot under the letter.

---

[1] The images are taken from Erdas Salci (ܣܠܓ̈ܐ) and İshak Akan (ܐܟܢ ܐܝܣܚܩ), ܣܘܪܝܝܐ ܣܦܪܐ (Södertälje, 1983).

The following image illustrates how to write the three words ܐܒ, ܓܒ, and ܕܐܘ. The numbers show the motions of the pen. An asterisk, *, indicates the beginning of a stroke, while a ' indicates the end of a stroke.

Let's start with ܐܒ. The ܐ is simply one stroke from point 1 to 2. Then ܒ is written as one stroke. You start from point 3, moving to 4 and 5, then continue up to point 6. Now, you continue to write over the same line but downward from point 6 through 7 ending at point 8. Remember, the whole of ܒ is one stroke.

The word ܓܒ is written with two strokes. In the first stroke, you write ܓ from point 1 to 2 then to 3. In the second stroke you write ܒ beginning at point 4 moving back and then down to point 3 to join with the first stroke, then moving to point 5. At point 5 you continue with the ܐ as in ܐܒ.

Let's move to ܕܐܘ. Two strokes take care of ܕ by following the points 1 through 6 for the first stroke, and then the dot at point 7 for the second stroke. Note that the connected dolath does not have a circular part on top of the writing line and hence there is nothing to fill. The ܐ is then straightforward (you can choose to make it straight or curved), then you write the ܘ as before.

Let's now turn our attention to the vowels. The following image gives the shapes of the

three vowels we covered.

The vowel Ỏ is written with two strokes as shown. The vowel Ȯ is written with one stroke, and the vowel Ö looks like an umbrella and is written with two strokes. Practice by putting them on the words ܐܒ, ܓܒ, and ܕܐܘ. Make sure to practice the writing many times before going to the next section. You may want to get some see-through paper and place it on top of the above examples, and trace over the letters and words.

Review

- The first four letters of the alphabet are: ܐ (Olaph, silent), ܒ (Béth, *b*), ܓ (Gomal, *g*), and ܕ (Dolath, *d*).
- Syriac is written from right to left.
- Some letters connect on both sides; others connect only on the right. The letters ܐ and ܕ connect only on the right, while ܒ and ܓ connect on both sides.
- The letter ܐ takes a straight shape when it precedes a letter, e.g., ܐܟܐ.
- The letter ܕ takes the shape ܖ when connected on the right; e.g., ܐܕܟ.
- Vowels are written above letters. Three (out of five) vowels are: ܘ̇ (*a*), ܘ̇ (*o*), and ܘ̇ (é).
- This section covered the following words:

father	ܐܒܐ
baby	ܚܒܐ
fruit	ܐܒܐ
uncle	ܐܘܕܐ
side	ܓܒܐ
bear	ܕܘܒܐ
was lost	ܐܒܕ
elected	ܓܒܐ
Baghdad	ܒܓܕܐܕ

Exercise

1. Transcribe in Syriac the following syllables:

    a. *ba*   b. *go*   c. *dé*   d. *o*

2. Translate the following into English:

    a. ܚܒܐ   b. ܐܒܕ   c. ܒܓܕܐܕ   d. ܓܒܐ

3. Put vowel marks on the following sentences:

    a. ܐܘܕ ܓܒܐ ܒܐܐ   b. ܐܘܕ ܐܒܐ ܓܒܐ

    c. ܐܒܐ ܐܒܕ

4. Translate the sentences in 3 into English.

.2 Hé, Waw, and Zayn

The next three letters of the Syriac alphabet are:

Name	Syriac	Hebrew	Arabic	Sound
Hé	ܗ	ה	ـه	h
Waw	ܘ	ו	و	w
Zayn	ܙ	ז	ز	z

Hé is pronounced as *h* in *home*, Waw as *w* in *we*, and Zayn as *z* in *zebra*. All three letters connect only to the right.

Another Vowel

In the previous section, we introduced three vowels: $\acute{o}$ (*a*), $\grave{o}$ (*o*), and $\tilde{o}$ (*é*). We are now ready to introduce a fourth vowel. Its name is ʿṣoṣo (again don't worry about the dots under 's' for now, or the first funny opening quote). What you need to know is its shape, $\acute{o}$, and its sound, *oo* as in *moon*.

Apart from two words which we will learn later (see section 1.4), $\acute{o}$ is always followed by the letter ܘ. In fact, the sequence ܘ$\acute{o}$ forms the vowel *oo*. Examples are: ܒܘ *boo*, ܓܘ *goo*, ܕܘ *doo*, ܗܘ *hoo*, etc.

The following table summarizes how the letters connect to each other.

	Final Position	Middle Position	Initial Position	Stand-alone Position
Hé	ܗܒ	ܒܗܒ	ܒܗ	ܗ
Waw	ܘܒ	ܒܘܒ	ܒܘ	ܘ
Zayn	ܙܒ	ܒܙܒ	ܒܙ	ܙ

Reading

Read the following with the aid of the CD. Try reading while covering the transliterations with a piece of paper.

ܗܘ	ܗ	ܗ	ܗ	1
hoo	hé	ho	ha	

ܘܿܘ	ܘ݂	ܘܿ	ܘܿ	2
woo	wé	wo	wa	

ܙܘܿ	ܙ݂	ܙܿ	ܙ݂	3
zoo	zé	zo	za	

English	Read	Syriac Word	
well (noun)	gu-bo	ܓܘܿܒܐ	4
bell	za-go	ܙܓܐ	5
goose	wa-zo	ܘܿܙܐ	6
treasure	ga-zo	ܓܙܐ	7
money, coin	zu-zo	ܙܘܿܙܐ	8
nut	gaw-zo	ܓܘܿܙܐ	9
flower	ha-bo-bo	ܗܿܒܒܐ	10
behold	ho	ܗܐ	11
that	haw	ܗܘܿ	12
he	hoo	ܗܘܿ	13
give (imperative)	hab	ܗܒ	14
inside	bgaw	ܒܓܘ	15

Phrases

ܘܿܙܐ	ܗܐ	1
goose	behold	

Behold! The goose.
Or: *Behold! A goose.*

ܙܘܿܙܐ	ܗܒ	ܐܒܐ	2
money	give	father	

Father, give money.

ܐܒ݂ܰܕ݂   ܓܰܐܙܳܐ   3
was lost   treasure

The treasure was lost.
Or: *A treasure was lost.*

ܓܰܘܙܳܐ   ܗܰܒ   ܕܳܕܳܐ   4
nut   give   uncle

Uncle, give a nut.

ܒܺܐܪܳܬ݂ܳܐ   ܓܰܘ   ܓܰܐܙܳܐ   5
well   inside treasure

The/a treasure inside the/a well.

Unlike English, Syriac does not have a clear DEFINITE ARTICLE (i.e., *the*), or INDEFINITE ARTICLE (i.e., *a/an*). So a sentence can be read both ways: *Behold! The goose*; or *Behold a goose*. Hopefully a larger context will give you a clue.

The Power of Waw

The letter ܘ also means *and*, but when it plays this role it attaches itself to the next word. Imagine the English sentence *cat and mouse* being written *cat andmouse* (without a space between *and* and *mouse*). For example, we can use ܘ with ܐܒ݂ܳܐ 'father' and ܒܢܳܐ 'child' as follows:

father and child	ܐܒ݂ܳܐ ܘܒܢܳܐ

Here are additional examples:

father and uncle	ܐܒ݂ܳܐ ܘܕܳܕܳܐ
treasure and money	ܓܰܐܙܳܐ ܘܙܽܘܙܳܐ
flower and nut	ܗܰܒܳܒ݂ܳܐ ܘܓܰܘܙܳܐ

Writing

The following images illustrate how to write ܗ, ܘ, and ܙ. The letter ܗ is written in two strokes. The tail in the first goes a bit below the writing line. Stroke 2 is clockwise in some traditions, but in others counter clockwise and begins at the point where the circle meets the tail. Similarly, ܘ is counter clockwise in some traditions. The tip of ܙ ends just under the writing line.

The following example illustrates how some of the letters of words we studied connect to each other.

The word ܠܐ is written in two strokes. In the first, the pen moves from 1 to 2, then to 3, then to 4 upwards. The pen then traces on the same line going down to point 5 and ends there. The second stroke is for the final ܐ.

The word ܗܘܐ is written in one stroke. When ܘ is connected, it is written clockwise.

The vowel Ȯ is written in two strokes, plus the dot as shown above.

Review

- We studied three more letters of the alphabet: ܗ (Hé, *h*), ܘ (Waw, *w*), and ܙ (Zayn, *z*). All three connect only to the right.
- We also covered the vowel Ȯ (*oo*) which is always followed by a ܘ.
- Syriac does not have a clear definite article (e.g., *the*) or indefinite article (i.e., *a/an*). Nouns can be translated either way depending on the context.

- The letter ‌ܘ‌ also means *and*. In such cases, it is attached to the word that follows it.
- This section covered the following new words:

behold	ܗܳܐ
that	ܗܰܘ
bell	ܙܰܓܳܐ
treasure	ܓܰܙܳܐ
flower	ܗܰܒܳܒܳܐ
he	ܗܽܘ
well (noun)	ܓܽܘܒܳܐ
goose	ܘܰܙܳܐ
money	ܙܽܘܙܳܐ
nut	ܓܰܘܙܳܐ
give (imperative)	ܗܰܒ
inside	ܓܰܘ

Exercise

1. Transcribe the following syllables in Syriac:

  a. *boo*   b. *zé*   c. *ha*   d. *wo*

  e. *woo*   f. *ga*   g. *zoo*   h. *zo*

2. Translate into English:

  a   ܗܳܐ ܘܰܙܳܐ ܘܗܰܒܳܒܳܐ

  b   ܘܰܙܳܐ ܘܓܰܙܳܐ ܗܰܒ ܠܓܽܘܒܳܐ

  c   ܐܰܒܳܐ ܗܰܘ ܗܰܒ ܓܰܘܙܳܐ

3. Translate into Syriac:

  a. Uncle, give money.

  b. The money was lost and the treasure was lost.

  c. The bear was lost inside the well.

4. Add vowel marks to the following sentences:

  a   ܐܒܐ ܗܘ ܪܒܐ

  b   ܗܐ ܓܒܐ ܐܒܝ

  c   ܗܘ ܐܒܐ ܓܒܐ ܘܘܐ

5. Translate the sentences in 4 into English.

3   Ḥéth, Ṭéth, and Yudh

This section introduces three additional letters. They are:

Name	Syriac	Hebrew	Arabic	Sound
Ḥéth	ܚ	ח	ح	ḥ
Ṭéth	ܛ	ט	ط	ṭ
Yudh	ܝ	י	ي	y

Now it is time to talk about the dots under letters!

There are sounds in Syriac that do not exist in English. We simply use the closest English sound with a dot under it to designate the sound. Both Ḥéth and Ṭéth are such sounds.

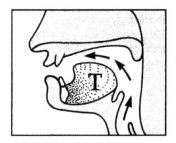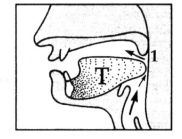

Figure 1. The pronounciation of *ḥ* (left) and ܚ (right).

The closest English sound to ܚ is *ḥ*, but it originates deeper in the throat as illustrated in Figure 1. Basically, you need to place the back of your tongue (designated by T in the diagrams) closer to point 1 in the diagram. Listen carefully to the CD in the reading sections to get the gist of it. The image above compares English *ḥ* (on the left) with ܚ (on the right).

The figure on the next page shows the sound of the letter ܛ (on the right) as compared with English *t* (on the left). In the case of *t*, you place the top of your tongue against your teeth; in the case of ܛ, however, you place the entire tongue on the roof of your mouth (point 1 in the figure on the next page). It is not easy if you have no prior experience in another Semitic language; you just need to practice.

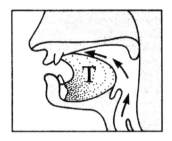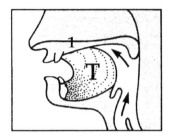

Figure 2. The pronunciation of *ṭ* (left) and ⸗ (right).

The letter ⸗ is simply pronounced as *y* in *yet*. Note that it is similar in shape to ⸗ and they can be easily confused—more on this below.

All three letters connect to both left and right. However, when ⸗ connects to a letter on the right, a stroke going from the base line to the top tip of the ⸗ makes that connection as in ⸗.

The following table summarizes how letters connect to each other.

	Final Position	Middle Position	Initial Position	Stand-alone Position
Ḥéth	⸗	⸗	⸗	⸗
Ṭéth	⸗	⸗	⸗	⸗
Yudh	⸗	⸗	⸗	⸗

One Final Vowel

We are ready now to introduce the last vowel. Its name is Ḥboṣo (again, don't worry about the name for now). Its shape is ⸗ and it is pronounced *ee* as in *meet*.

Usually, but not always, ⸗ is followed by Yudh when it forms this vowel as in ⸗ (the same way ⸗ is usually followed by o to form o⸗). For example, ⸗ reads *hee*.

Reading

Read the following with the aid of the CD. Pay special attention to the pronunciation of ⸗ and ⸗.

⸗	⸗	⸗	⸗	⸗	1
Ḥoo	Ḥee	Ḥé	Ḥo	Ḥa	

Ṭoo	Ṭee	Ṭé	Ṭo	Ṭa	2
Yoo	Yee	Yé	Yo	Ya	3
Ḥoo	Ḥee	Ḥé	Ḥo	Ḥa	4
Ṭoo	Ṭee	Ṭé	Ṭo	Ṭa	5
Yoo	Yee	Yé	Yo	Ya	6

English	Read	Syriac Word	
hand	ee-do	أَمِرا	7
good	ṭo-bo	لُخا	8
thread	ḥoo-ṭo	شَوكِا	9
duck	ba-ṭo	حَكِا	10
saw (to see)	ḥzo	سِرا	11
sinned	ḥṭo	سكِا	12
one (masc.)	ḥad	مَبِ	13
one (fem.)	ḥdo	سِرا	14

Masculine and Feminine

Did you notice that both مَبِ and سِرا mean *one*? The first is designated as masculine and the second as feminine. While numbers in English are not gender-specific (masculine versus feminine), they are in Syriac.

Nouns are also classified as masculine or feminine. The nouns we have listed above (apart from إِيدَا 'hand') are all masculine. When words modify each other, they must have the same gender. For example, we say إِيدَا أَمِدَا 'one hand' (both words are feminine), but أَبَا حَدَ 'one father' (both words are masculine).

Recognizing feminine words is not as bad as it looks because most of them end in a letter called *Taw*. But as it is the last letter of the alphabet, you just have to wait until we learn it.

Beware of ܚ Next to ܝ

As mentioned above, the shape of ܚ is similar to ܝ and they can be easily confused. Can you read this word: ܝܚܝܕܐ?

Here it is again with vowels: ܝܺܚܝܕܳܐ. Does that help?

Now, here it is with longer connections between the letters: ܝܺܚܝܕܳܐ. So the first letter is ܝ (Yudh), the second is ܚ (Ḥeth) and the third is ܝ (Yudh). The word ܝܺܚܝܕܳܐ (get used to it without the longer connections) means *single* or *solitary*. It is also a reference to Christ as the *only-begotten*.

Phrases

أَمِدَا	مِزَا	أَحَا	1
hand	saw	brother	

The/a brother saw the/a hand.

حَبَا گَوَ بِزَا	وَإِوَزَا	بَطَا	هَا	2
well	inside	and+goose	duck	behold	

Behold, the duck and the goose inside the well.

طَبَا	وَدَدَا	طَبَا	أَحَا	3
good	and+uncle	good	brother	

Good brother and good uncle.

حَبَا گَوَ بِزَا	گَزَا	مِزَا	أَبَا	4
well	inside	treasure	saw	father	

The father saw the treasure inside the well.

سَنِّ   عَمّوً   5

sinned   uncle

The uncle sinned.

Writing

Each of the letters introduced in this section is written in one stroke as shown below. Note that ــس and ــس are similar. (Note that there are two ways to begin ــس and ــس. The first is as shown in ــس at point 1 where you start at the circle, move a bit up, then down and to the right. The second is as in ــس at point 1.)

Here are a few words that illustrate how letters connect with each other. The word أَبِاً is written in four strokes. First you write أ as before. Then you write ــب from point 3, moving to point 4, then tracing down to point 5, in addition to the dot at point 6. Then you write the final أ which is straight.

The word شَمّوً is written in two strokes. First ــم is written following points 1 to 9. You start at point 1 at the writing line, then move a bit above the line to point 2, then back to the writing line at point 3. You repeat the same process going to point 4, then 5. Now you continue to point six to write the o ending at point 9. The second stroke is for لُ. You start from the top at point 10, moving down to point 11, then counter clockwise to point 12 and continuing the circle and moving to point 13. From point 13, you write the final ا as you learned in the previous lesson, going to the top of the letter, then tracing on the same line to the bottom.

Finally, ܟ݂ܶ is written in one stroke. You start from point 1, back to the writing line at point 2, then finishing the ܒ at point 3. Now you go up to connect to the top of the ܛ at point 4. You then move down to point 5. From point 5, you follow the same steps as you did with ܛܳܘ to finish the word.

The vowel ܳ is written in three strokes as indicated. You can interchange the order of strokes 1 and 2.

Review

- We studied three more letters of the alphabet: ܚ (Ḥéth, ḥ), ܛ (Ṭéth, ṭ), and ܝ (Yudh, y). The first two letters do not have equivalent sounds in English (see above for more details.)
- All three connect to the left and the right, but ܛ takes a long stroke from the base line to its top tip when it connects to preceding letters, e.g., ܒܛ.
- We also covered the vowel ܳ (ee) which is often followed by a ܝ.
- Nouns in Syriac are classified as either feminine or masculine. Unless otherwise stated, you can assume that the nouns we introduce are masculine.
- Special attention must be paid in order not to confuse adjacent ܝ and ܚ ; e.g., ܡܣܲܝܒܰܐ .
- This section covered the following new words:

hand (feminine)	ܐܺܝܕ݂ܳܐ
brother	ܐܰܚܳܐ
good	ܛܳܒ݂ܳܐ
thread	ܚܽܘܛܳܐ
duck	ܒܰܛܳܐ

saw (past tense of *to see*)	ܡܙܐ
sinned	ܣܟܠܐ
one (masculine)	ܚܰܕ
one (feminine)	ܚܕܐ
single, solitary, only-begotten	ܝܺܚܝܕܳܝܐ

Vocabulary Review

All the words we have learned before are listed here in alphabetical order:

father	ܐܰܒܐ
fruit	ܐܷܒܐ
was lost	ܐܷܒܶܕ
brother	ܐܰܚܐ
hand (f.)	ܐܝܕܐ
baby	ܚܬܐ
Baghdad	ܒܰܓܕܐܕ
inside	ܓܰܘܶܗ
duck	ܒܰܛܐ
elected	ܓܒܐ
side	ܓܒܐ
well (noun)	ܓܘܒܐ
nut	ܓܘܙܐ
treasure	ܓܰܙܐ
bear	ܕܘܒܐ
uncle	ܕܘܕܐ
behold	ܗܐ
give (imperative)	ܗܒ
flower	ܗܒܒܐ
he	ܗܘ
that	ܗܘ
goose	ܘܙܐ
bell	ܙܓܐ

money ܙܽܘܙܳܐ

single, solitary, only-begotten ܝܺܚܺܝܕܳܝܳܐ

one (m.) ܚܰܕ

one (f.) ܚܕܳܐ

thread ܚܽܘܛܳܐ

saw (past tense of *to see*) ܚܙܳܐ

sinned ܚܛܳܐ

good ܛܳܒܳܐ

Exercise

1. Translate into English:

a ܐܰܒܳܐ ܚܙܳܐ ܚܰܕ ܚܽܘܛܳܐ ܒܓܰܘ ܓܽܘܒܳܐ

b ܚܰܕ ܒܰܛܳܐ ܐܰܒܰܕ

c ܐܰܒܳܐ ܚܛܳܐ ܘܕܳܕܳܐ ܚܛܳܐ

2. Translate into Syriac:

   a. A good uncle sinned.

   b. One hand, and one good duck.

   c. The good uncle* saw a goose inside the well.

   * Hint: Look at sentence 3 above for the word order for *good uncle* (the adjective follows the noun).

3. Put vowel marks on the following:

a ܗܘ ܐܒܐ ܚܙܐ ܐܡܐ ܒܒܐ

b ܗܐ ܐܒܐ ܘܕܕܐ ܛܒܐ

c ܚܕ ܐܒܐ

d ܚܕܐ ܐܝܕܐ

4. Translate the sentences in 3 into English.

4   Koph, Lomadh, Mim, and Nun

This section introduces the next four letters of the Syriac alphabet. They are:

Name	Syriac	Hebrew	Arabic	Sound
Koph	ܟ	כ	ك	k
Lomadh	ܠ	ל	ل	l
Mim	ܡ	מ	م	m
Nun	ܢ	ן	ن	n

The letter ܟ sounds like *k* in *kilo*, ܠ as *l* in *let*, ܡ as *m* in *meet*, and ܢ as *n* in *not*.

There are two things that are unique about this set of letters. Firstly, their sequence in the alphabet corresponds to the sequence of their counterparts in the English alphabet, so it is easier to remember their sequence: *k*, *l*, *m*, *n*.

Secondly, each of the above letters has two shapes. One used in the beginning and middle of words, and the other at the end of words. The forms shown above are the final forms that appear at the end of words. The forms that appear at the beginning and middle of words are:

Koph   ܒ

Lomadh   ܠ

Mim   ܡ

Nun   ܢ

The following table summarizes how these letters connect to others.

	Final Position	Middle Position	Initial Position	Stand-alone Position
Koph	ܟ	ܟܟܟ	ܟܟ	ܟ
Lomadh	ܠ	ܠܠܠ	ܠܠ	ܠ
Mim	ܡ	ܡܡܡ	ܡܡ	ܡ
Nun	ܢ	ܢܢܢ	ܢܢ	ܢ

One more thing before we move on… No two letters of the alphabet are more envious of each other than ܐ (whose shape is straight up) and ܠ (whose shape is slanted like a back slash, \). How so?

Well, if ܐ is immediately followed by ܠ, it gets envious and wants to be slanted too. So you end up with ܠܐ instead of ܠܐ.

Now, if ܠ is immediately followed by ܐ, it too gets envious and wants to be straight up. So you end up with ܠܐ instead of ܠܐ.

In other words, whichever letter comes first, it assumes the shape of the following letter. Here are two examples:

no   ܠܐ

God   ܐܠܗܐ

While ܠܐ is obligatory, ܠܐ is optional. So one can still write ܐܠܗܐ.

Reading

koo	kee	ké	ko	ka	1
loo	lee	lé	lo	la	2
moo	mee	mé	mo	ma	3
noo	nee	né	no	na	4
					5
					6
					7
					8

English	Read	Syriac Word	
mother (f.)	é-mo	أَمُلا	9
fish	nu-no	نُوَلا	10
this (m.)	ho-no	هُولا	11
this (f.)	ho-dé	هُوْدِا	12
sea	ya-mo	يَمُلا	13
camel	ga-mlo	كَمْلا	14
milk	ḥal-bo	حَلْبُلا	15
salt	mél-ḥo	مِلْحُلا	16
I	é-no	أَلا	17
God	a-lo-ho	الَهُولا	18
spoke	ma-lel	مَلِلْ	19
ate	é-kal	أَكَلْ	20
went	é-zal	أَزَلْ	21
from	men	مِنْ	22
every, each	kul	كُلْ	23
because	me-ṭul	مِطُلْ	24

Where Did the Waw Go?

I mentioned earlier in section 1.2 that whenever there is the vowel $\acute{o}$, it is always followed by ܘ. There are two words that violate this rule. They are ܟܠ 'every' and ܡܛܠ 'because'. In fact, in early Syriac manuscripts, even these two words appear with a ܘ as in ܟܘܠ and ܡܛܘܠ. (Some contemporary educators, in particular Abrohom Nuro, call for bringing back the old tradition of using ܘ in these two words.)

Phrases

	ܢܘܢܐ	ܕܝܟ	ܝܰܡܐ	1
	sea	in	fish	

The fish in the sea.

	ܐܟܠ	ܓܡܠܐ	ܗܢܐ	ܐܟܠ	2
	fruit	ate	camel	this	

This camel ate fruit.

	ܒܓܕܐܕ	ܡܢ	ܘܚܠܒܐ	ܡܠܚܐ	3
	Baghdad from	and+milk	salt	

Salt and milk from Baghdad.

	ܘܐܙܠ	ܡܠܠ	ܕܕܐ	4
	and+went	spoke	uncle	

The uncle spoke and went.

	ܓܘܙܐ	ܐܟܠ	ܕܒܐ	ܟܠ	5
	nut	ate	bear	each	

Each bear ate a nut.

Writing

Recall that each of the letters introduced in this section has two shapes: one used in the beginning and middle of words, and another at the end. Here are the various shapes:

Initial ܕ and final ܩ are written in one stroke. There is actually another tradition of writing final ܩ in two strokes: you first write a ܢ, then write the tail under it to make ܩ. (The

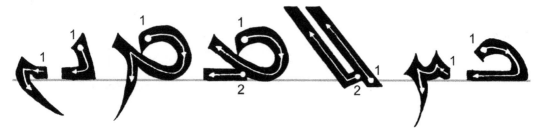

one stroke tradition prevails in Tur Abdin.) The letter ܠ is written in two strokes as shown; its initial version ܠ is also written in two strokes where the second stroke is simply the connecting line. This will be illustrated in the example below. Initial ܡ is written in two strokes, the second stroke being the connection line, while final ܡ is written in one stroke. Finally, initial ܪ and final ܥ are written in one stroke.

Here are some word examples. Remember that * marks a new stroke, and ' marks the end of a stroke.

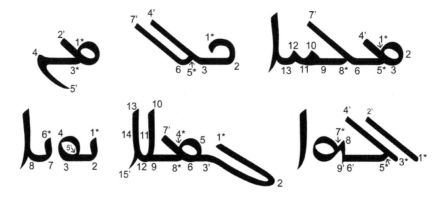

The word ܡܫܠܝܐ is written in three strokes. You begin writing ܡ from point 1 to 4 in one stroke, then write its connection line starting at point 5 with a second stroke. The second stroke continues in writing the slanted portion of the letter ܠ ending at point 7. The third stroke begins at point 8 writing the connection line for ܠ and then continues to write ܝ. Once at point 13, you write the final ܠ as before moving the pen to the top of the letter, then tracing on the same line to the bottom.

The word ܟܠ is written in two strokes. In the first stroke, you write ܟ starting from point 1, passing through point 2, then moving to point 3. With the same stroke you start writing ܠ and end the stroke at the top of the letter at point 4. You then start the second stroke at point 5, moving to point 6 then 7.

The word ܡܢ is written in two strokes. The ܡ is written the same way as ܡ in ܫܡܠܝܐ. Then the final ܢ is written as shown above.

The rest of the words are written tracing the points as indicated. Note that ܠܗܐ has the ligature ܠܠ and ܡܠܠ has the ligature ܠܠ. The latter is written like final ܠ where you begin at the bottom of the ligature (point 9 in ܡܠܠ) moving up to point 10, then tracing down on the same line to point 12, then moving up to point 13, then tracing down on the same line through point 14 ending in point 15.

Review

- We introduced three more letters of the alphabet: ܟ (Koph, *k*), ܠ (Lomadh, *l*), ܡ (Mim, *m*), and ܢ (Nun, *n*). All four connect on both sides.
- All four letters have another shape that is used at the beginning and middle of words: ܟ (Koph), ܠ (Lomadh), ܡ (Mim), and ܢ (Nun).
- When ܠ is followed by ܐ, it becomes straight (e.g., ܠܐ); when ܐ is followed by ܠ, it *optionally* becomes slanted (e.g., ܐܠܗܐ).
- This section covered the following new words:

mother	ܐܡܐ
fish	ܢܘܢܐ
this (m.)	ܗܢܐ
this (f.)	ܗܕܐ
sea	ܝܡܐ
camel	ܓܡܠܐ
milk	ܚܠܒܐ
salt	ܡܠܚܐ
I	ܐܢܐ
God	ܐܠܗܐ
spoke	ܡܠܠ

ate	ܐܰܟ݂ܶܠ
went	ܐܶܙܰܠ
from	ܡܶܢ
all	ܟܽܠ
because	ܡܶܛܽܠ

Exercise

1. Translate into English:

   ܐܰܟ݂ܳܐ ܐܰܟ݂ܶܠ ܗ݇ܘܳܐ ܐܰܝܟ݂ ܗ݇ܘܳܐ   a

   ܗܳܢܳܐ ܙܽܘܙܳܐ ܣܳܪܳܐ ܗܳܕܳܐ ܕܶܝܢ ܝܰܡܳܐ   b

   ܐܰܟ݂ܳܐ ܣܰܠܳܐ ܗ݇ܘܳܕܶ   c

2. Translate into Syriac:

   a. This father, and this mother.

   b. God spoke.

   c. This milk from Baghdad.

3. Write the number 'one' in Syriac in the following:

   ܐܳܒ݂ܳܐ _____   a

   ܐܶܡܳܐ _____   b

   ܐܰܪܳܐ _____   c

   ܐܰܠܳܗܳܐ _____   d

4. Put vowel marks on the following:

   ܗܘ ܐܒܐ ܐܙܠ   a

   ܗܘܐ ܐܡܐ   b

   ܗܘ ܝܡܠܐ ܐܡܠ   c

   ܐܢܐ ܗܘܘ   d

5. Translate the sentences in 4 into English.

5   The ܒܕܘܠ Letters

Do you remember the Power of Waw?

Recall from section 1.2 that the letter ܘ, which means *and*, attaches itself to the next word. For example, ܘ attached to ܝܰܠܕܳܐ 'child' gives ܘܝܰܠܕܳܐ 'and child'.

Three other letters operate in the same way: they attach themselves to the following word. Here they are listed along with ܘ:

ܒ	meaning *in*	ܕ	meaning *of*
ܘ	meaning *and*	ܠ	meaning *to*

The four letters are known as 'the ܒܕܘܠ letters.' (They have meanings other than the ones listed above depending on the context in which they occur.) Let us look at some examples.

ܐܰܒܳܐ	ܒܒܰܓܕܰܐܕ	1
father	in+Baghdad	

The father in Baghdad.

ܢܽܘܢܳܐ	ܕܝܰܡܳܐ	2
fish	of+sea	

The fish of the sea.

ܓܰܙܳܐ	ܕܰܐܒܳܐ	ܘܕܳܕܳܐ	3
treasure	of+father	and+uncle	

The treasure of the father and the uncle.

ܙܽܘܙܳܐ	ܕܰܐܒܳܐ	ܐܰܒܰܕ	ܒܓܽܘܒܳܐ	4
Money	of+father	lost	in+well	

The money of the father was lost in the well.

ܗܳܐ	ܓܰܙܳܐ	ܒܓܽܘܒܳܐ	5
behold	treasure	in+well	

Behold! The treasure in the well.

ܐܰܒܳܐ	ܗܰܒ	ܙܽܘܙܳܐ	ܠܕܳܕܳܐ	6
father	give	money	to+uncle	

Father, give money to uncle.

Inserting An ◌ܰ

Try reading the following words:

and chose	ܘܓܒܳܐ
in one	ܒܚܕܳܐ
of one	ܕܚܕܳܐ

You will find that it is not easy to read such words because the words begin with three letters without a vowel in between. To resolve this problem, Syriac adds an ◌ܰ vowel on the ܒܘܟܠ letter as follows:

and chose	ܘܰܓܒܳܐ
in one	ܒܰܚܕܳܐ
of one	ܕܰܚܕܳܐ

If the word, however, has a vowel on the first letter such as ܕܳܕܳܐ or ܪܽܘܙܳܐ then we simply add the ܒܘܟܠ letter without a vowel; e.g., ܘܕܳܕܳܐ, ܠܕܳܕܳܐ, ܕܪܽܘܙܳܐ.

Olaph is Too Lazy to Hold a Vowel!

Olaph does not like carrying a vowel, especially at the beginning of a word. It is just too much work for Olaph! So as soon as one of the ܒܘܟܠ letters joins a word that begins with Olaph, Olaph throws its vowel to the ܒܘܟܠ letter. For example, ܐܰܒܳܐ 'father', ܘܰܐܒܳܐ 'and father' (not ܘܐܰܒܳܐ). Similarly, ܐܶܙܰܠ 'went', ܘܶܐܙܰܠ 'and went' (not ܘܐܶܙܰܠ).

By the way… this rule applies only to West Syriac. In East Syriac, Olaph retains the vowel.

More than One ܒܘܟܠ

More than one ܒܘܟܠ letter can be attached to words. For example,

sea	ܝܰܡܳܐ
in the sea	ܒܝܰܡܳܐ
and in the sea	ܘܰܒܝܰܡܳܐ

Note that we added an ◌ܰ on the ܘ as described in the previous section because ܒ does not have a vowel on it.

Review

- The four letters known as ܒܕܘܠ (i.e., ܒ 'in', ܕ 'of', ܘ 'and', and ܠ 'to') act as prefixes.

- When a word begins with an unvocalized letter, the vowel ̊ is placed on top of the ܒܕܘܠ letter (e.g., ܚܰܕ 'one', ܘܚܰܕ 'and one').

- If the word begins with an ܐ with a vowel, the vowel moves to the ܒܕܘܠ letter (e.g., ܐܰܒܳܐ 'father', ܘܐܰܒܳܐ 'and the father'; ܐܶܡܳܐ 'mother', ܕܐܶܡܳܐ 'of the mother').

- More than one ܒܕܘܠ letter may be attached to a word (e.g., ܘܒܓܘܒܳܐ 'and in the well').

Exercise

1. Translate into English:

$$\text{ܘܗܽܘ ܟܡܰܠ ܐܰܚܳܐ ܘܐܳܪܒ} \qquad \text{a}$$

$$\text{ܘܗܺܝ ܘܐܰܚܳܐ ܠܐܰܚܳܐ ܣܪܳܐ ܟܪܳܐ ܚܟܺܝܳܐܘ} \qquad \text{b}$$

$$\text{ܐܰܚܳܐ ܐܰܚܳܐ ܢܗܳܠ ܘܗܘܳܘ} \qquad \text{c}$$

2. Translate into Syriac:

a. And the father of the baby went to Baghdad.

b. The uncle went and elected the mother.

c. The father went because the uncle elected the mother.

.6   Simkath, ʿé, Phé, and Ṣodhé

This section introduces the next four letters of the Syriac alphabet. They are:

Name	Syriac	Hebrew	Arabic	Sound
Simkath	ܣ	ס	س	s
ʿé	ܥ	ע	ع	(see below)
Phé	ܦ	פ	ف	f
Ṣodhé	ܨ	צ	ص	ṣ

The letter ܣ sounds like *s* in *sand*, and ܦ sounds like *f* in *fat*. The two other letters do not have an exact sound in English.

The sound of the letter ܥ is the hardest to master as there is no corresponding, or even close, sound in English. The sound is achieved by closing the glottal (point 1 in Figure 3). Listen very carefully to the CD.

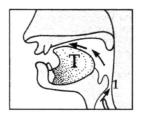

Figure 3. The pronounciation of ܥ.

The shape of ܥ is similar to ܠ, but is shorter. Like ܠ, the letter ܥ has two forms. The first is used at the beginning of words, ܥـ; the second is used at the end of words, ܥ. The letter ܥ is usually transliterated in the Roman alphabet by an open single quote ʿ or a similar symbol like ʿ which we will use in this book. Sometimes you see it transliterated as a small superscript ᶜ, or something similar.

The letter ܨ sounds like *s* but with the tip of the tongue against the roof of the mouth (point 1 in Figure 4), rather than the teeth, and by opening your mouth more. It connects only to the right.

Figure 4. The pronounciation of *s* (left) and ܨ (right).

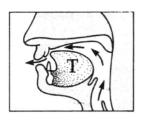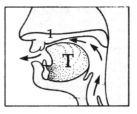

The following table summarizes how these letters connect to others.

	Final Position	Middle Position	Initial Position	Stand-alone Position
Simkath	ܣܒ	ܣܒܣ	ܣܒ	ܣ
ʿé	ܥܒ	ܥܒܢ	ܥܒ	ܥ
Phe	ܦܒ	ܦܒܣ	ܦܒ	ܦ
Ṣodhe	ܨ	ܨ	ܨ	ܨ

Reading

Listen to the CD. Pay attention to the sound of ܥ (line 2) and ܨ (line 4). Also, compare the sounds in lines 4 and 5 to distinguish between ܣ and ܨ. I am providing the transliteration for lines 1 and 2 only.

soo	see	sé	so	sa	1
ʿoo	ʿee	ʿé	ʿo	ʿa	2
					3
					4
					5
					6
					7
					8

English	Read	Syriac Word	
world	ʿol-mo	ܥܳܠܡܳܐ	9
worlds	ʿol-mé	ܥܳܠܡ̈ܐ	10
people	ʿa-mo	ܥܰܡܳܐ	11
peoples	ʿa-mé	ܥܰܡ̈ܐ	12
law	no-moo-so	ܢܳܡܘܿܣܳܐ	13
laws	no-moo-sé	ܢܳܡܘܿܣ̈ܐ	14
slave, servant	ʿab-do	ܥܰܒܕܳܐ	15
slaves, servants	ʿab-dé	ܥܰܒܕ̈ܐ	16
ground	ar-ʿo	ܐܰܪܥܳܐ	17
please!	bbo-ʿoo	ܒܒܳܥܘܿ	18
on	ʿal	ܥܰܠ	19
desired	ṣbo	ܨܒܳܐ	20
wanted, asked for	bʿo	ܒܥܳܐ	21
fell	nfal	ܢܦܰܠ	22

What are Those Two Dots?

You probably have noticed the two dots above some words. The dots mark plurals, and are called in Syriac ܣܝ̈ܡܐ *syomé* (itself a plural).

There are many rules for forming plurals. The simplest rule applies to most masculine nouns ending with ܐܳ. Simply, replace the final ܳ with ̈ and add the two-dot *syomé*. For example, ܥܳܠܡܳܐ 'world' becomes ܥܳܠܡ̈ܐ 'worlds'.

Where does one place the two-dot *syomé*? In older manuscripts, *syomé* tended to be towards the end of the word. But there are really no rules. You can put it anywhere as in ܢܳܡܘ̈ܣܐ, ܢܳܡ̈ܘܣܐ, ܢ̈ܡܘܣܐ 'laws'. Myself, I prefer to put it on a letter that does not have a vowel as in ܢܳܡܘ̈ܣܐ. Also, I try to avoid placing it above tall letters such as ܐ, ܠ, or ܛ.

Phrases

1 ܐܰܒܳܐ ܨܒܳܐ ܟܶܣܦܳܐ ܡܶܢ ܕܳܕܳܐ

      father   wanted   money   from   uncle

The father wanted money from the uncle.

2 ܕܺܒܳܐ ܢܦܰܠ ܥܰܠ ܐܰܪܥܳܐ

      bear   fell   on   ground

The bear fell on the ground.

3 ܢܳܡܽܘܣܳܐ ܕܥܰܡܳܐ ܠܳܐ ܢܳܡܽܘܣܳܐ ܕܥܰܡܡܶܐ

      laws   of+people   not   law   of+peoples

The laws of the people, not the law of the peoples.

4 ܐܶܢܳܐ ܥܰܒܕܳܐ ܕܰܐܠܳܗܳܐ

      I   servant   of+God

I (am) the servant of God

5 ܫܐܶܠ ܥܰܒܕܳܐ ܡܶܢ ܐܰܠܳܗܳܐ

      asked   servant   from   God

The servant asked of God.

Writing

The following image shows how the letters introduced in this section are written.

The letter ܣ is written in one stroke. The stroke starts at the middle of the letter at point 1, moves clockwise to complete the first circle, then with the same stroke the second circle is written closing it at point 1, then tracing on the same line under the second circle to get to the end of the letter. The examples below illustrate this more clearly with various point marks on the letter.

The letter ܥ is written with two strokes similar to the letter ܨ. The letters ܦ and ܩ are also written with one stroke each. Note that ܩ is mostly under the writing line.

Here are some writing examples.

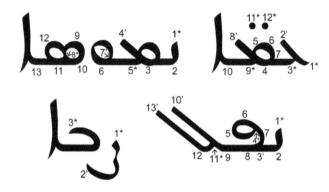

The word ܚܳܛܳܐ is written in three strokes, in addition to the *syomé*. The first stroke is for the slanted portion of ܟ from point 1 to 2. The second stroke begins at point 3 for the connection line of ܟ then moves to point 4 and begins writing the letter ܣ, drawing a circle clockwise passing through points 5, 6, and 7, then back to point 4, then up to point 8 where the stroke ends. The third stroke starts at point 9 connecting ܣ to the final ܠ and ends after writing ܠ as before. Then you write the *syomé* dots, first the left dot then the right dot (yes, that is correct, first *left* then *right*).

The word ܪܣܘܡܐ is also written in three strokes. The first begins at point 1 for ܪ, passes through point 2, then to point 3. At point three, you draw the circle of ܣ clockwise as you did in ܚܳܛܳܐ before ending the first stroke at point 4. I did not put all the points for you for ܣ; follow the points in ܚܳܛܳܐ. The second stroke starts at point 5 and connects the ܣ to the ܘ. At point 6, you draw the ܘ clockwise ending at point 7. The third final stroke is for writing ܡܐ. It begins in the middle of ܡ at point 8, then moves clockwise to points 9 and 10. Then you move to point 11 and start clockwise writing the second circle of ܡ passing through point 12, and then point 8 again. Then you continue through point 11 again. Finally, you move to point 13 and finish the final ܠ.

The word ܦܠ is also written in three strokes. In the first you write ܠ (points 1 to 3). In the second you write ܦ and the the first line of ܠ. This stroke begins at point 4, then passes through points 5, 6, and 7. Before you get to point 8, you pass through point 3 again. From point 8, you move to point 9 then 10. The final stroke finishes ܠ starting at point 11, through 12 to 13.

Finally, ܠܕ is written in two strokes. The ܕ is simply written by tracing from point 1 to 2. ܠ is written as before.

Review

- We introduced four more letters of the alphabet: ܣ (Simkath, *s*), ܥ (ʿE), ܦ (Phe, *f*), and ܨ (Ṣodhé, *ṣ*). The first three letters connect on both sides; ܨ connects only to the right.

- Plurals are marked with two dots called *syomé* as in ܥܰܒ̈ܕܶܐ 'servants'. The simplest rule of making plurals, which applies to many masculine nouns, is changing the final ܐܳ to ܐܶ̈ as in ܓܰܙܳܐ 'treasure', ܓܰܙܶܐ̈ 'treasures'.

- This section covered the following new words:

world	ܥܳܠܡܳܐ
people	ܥܰܡܳܐ
law	ܢܳܡܘܿܣܳܐ
slave, servant	ܥܰܒܕܳܐ
ground	ܐܰܪܥܳܐ
please!	ܒܳܥܶܐܢܐ
on	ܥܰܠ
desired	ܪܓܳܐ
wanted, asked	ܒܥܳܐ
fell	ܢܦܰܠ

Exercise

1. Translate into English:

a   ܐܰܪܥܳܐ ܥܰܠ ܢܦܰܠ ܥܰܒܕܳܐ

b   ܒܳܥܶܐܢܐ ܗܘ ܐܙܳܠ ܘܐܳܡܰܪ ܗܘ

c ܗܵܘܢܵܐ ܚܲܒ݂ܪܵܐ ܚܲܕ݂ ܥܲܒ݂ܕܵܐ ܡܸܢ ܐܲܟ݂ܵܐ

2. Translate into Syriac:

 a. This world.

 b. Please give me (ܠܝܼ) money and treasure.

 c. The servants of God, and not the servant of the peoples.

3. Form the plural for the following words:

 a. ܐܸܡܵܐ b. ܟܲܟ݂ܕ݂ܵܐ c. ܘܲܪܕܵܐ d. ܩܵܪܵܐ

 e. ܚܲܒ݂ܪܵܐ

4. Form the singular of the following words:

 a. ܛܵܠܵܝ̈ܐ b. ܘܲܪ̈ܕܐ c. ܥܲܒ݂ܕܹ̈ܐ d. ܩܵܩܘܵܬܼ̈ܐ

7   Qoph, Rish, Shin, and Taw

This section introduces the last four letters of the Syriac alphabet. They are:

Name	Syriac	Hebrew	Arabic	Sound
Qoph	ܩ	ק	ق	close to q
Rish	ܪ	ר	ر	r
Shin	ܫ	שׁ	ش	sh
Taw	ܬ	ת	ت	t

The letter ܩ does not have a similar sound in English, and is hard to master. Say *k* and notice where the back of your tongue touches the roof of your mouth (point 1 in Figure 5). Now say *q* and notice that you have lowered the point where the back of your tongue

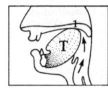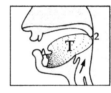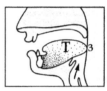

Figure 5. The pronounciation of *k* (left), *q* (middle) and ܩ (right).

touches the roof of your mouth (point 2). Now—get some cough syrup and—try to go ten times lower (point 3), hopefully without irritating your throat! The letter ܩ is transliterated in Roman letters as *q*, the closest sound to it.

The letter ܪ sounds like *r* but rolled the Scottish way. Note that ܪ looks exactly the same as ܕ except that the dot is on top of the letter. Similar to ܕ, it takes another shape when connected to the previous letter as in ܒܪ. It does not connect to the left.

The letter ܫ sounds like *sh* in *shame*. It connects on both sides.

Finally, the letter ܬ sounds like *t* in *tea*. When ܬ connects to the previous letter, a stroke that goes from the baseline to the top of the ܬ makes the connection, as in ܒܬ (similar to the line that connects ܒܠ). It does not connect to the left.

The following table summarizes how these letters connect to others.

	Final Position	Middle Position	Initial Position	Stand-alone Position
Qoph	ܩ	ܩܩ	ܩܕ	ܩ
Rish	ܪ	ܪܕ	ܘܕ	ܪ
Shin	ܫ	ܫܫ	ܫܕ	ܫ
Taw	ܬ	ܬܬ	ܬܐ	ܬ

Reading

The first line is transliterated for you. Follow the same vowel patterns in lines 2-4.

ܩܘ	ܩܹ	ܩܹ	ܩܿ	ܩܲ	1
Qoo	Qee	Qé	Qo	Qa	

| ܪܘ | ܪܹ | ܪ | ܪ | ܪ | 2 |

| ܫܘ | ܫܹ | ܫ | ܫ | ܫ | 3 |

| ܬܘ | ܬܹ | ܬ | ܬ | ܬ | 4 |

English	Read	Syriac Word	
high	ro-mo	ܪܳܡܐ	5
big	ra-bo	ܪܰܒܐ	6
now	ho-sho	ܗܳܫܐ	7
sister	ḥo-tho	ܚܳܬܐ	8
Christ	m-shi-ḥo	ܡܫܝܚܐ	9
Lord	mor-yo	ܡܳܪܝܐ	10
spirit	roo-ḥo	ܪܘܚܐ	11
holy	qa-dee-sho	ܩܰܕܝܫܐ	12
true	sha-ree-ro	ܫܰܪܝܪܐ	13
said	é-mar	ܐܡܲܪ	14

went out	n-faq	نَقَم 15
son	b-ro	حَزُا 16
name	sh-mo	معمُا 17

Phrases

	ەوُحزُا	وِأحُا	حَمعُا 1
	and+of+son	of+father	in+name

In the name of the Father, and of the Son…

أنَمزُا حَدُّهُا	مَبِ	مَّبِّعُا	ەوُوُهمُا 2
true	God	one	holy	and+of+spirit

… and of the Holy Spirit, one true God.

مُدنُا حَدُّهُا 3	
God	Lord

Lord God!

محمُسُا حزُا وِحَدُّهُا أحُا 4			
father	of+God	son	Christ

Christ, Son of God the Father.

حَدمُا وُحُا ەوُمُا 5			
and+tall	big	house	

A big and tall house.

Writing

The following graph illustrates how the letters of this section are written. The letter ڡ is written with one stroke as shown. The letter ؛ is written like ؛ but with the dot on the top; remember the top portion has to be filled in a clockwise movement. The letter ۻ, as written by the calligrapher below, is made of two strokes. I learned how to write it in one stroke by connecting both strokes at point 2, and filling out the interior of the letter in a counter clockwise, spiral motion, with each circile starting at point 2, and finally making the connection line also starting at point 2. The letter ﻝ is written in one stroke from top to bottom.

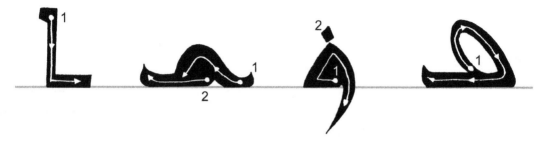

Here are some examples that illustrate how to write a few words. The word ﻟﺤﺎ is written in three strokes. The first two are for the letter ﻭ as we learned before (first stroke from point 1 to 2, and the second stroke from point 3 drawing a circle counter clockwise, or clockwise according to other traditions, back to point 3). The third stroke is for ﻟﺤ. Start at point 4, up to point 5, then point 6, then point 7, then back to somewhere between points 7 and 4 to close the gap. Now fill in the ﺤ in a counter clockwise movement. When you are done filling it, you should be at point 4. Now move to point 8, and draw the final ﻝ as before.

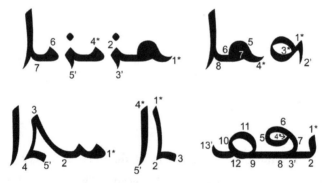

The word ﻟﺜﻘﻰ is written in three strokes: the first for ﻘﻰ, the second for ﺜ and the third for ﻝ. Simply follow the points as before.

The word ﻳﻘﻒ is written in two strokes: the first for ﺭ from point 1 to 2 to 3, then the second for ﻳﻖ starting at point 4. You then move clockwise to point 5, then 6, then 7, then 8 (passing through point 3 again), then 9. Now you continue with the same stroke in clockwise motion to point 10, 11, then 12 (passing by point 9 again), and finishing at point 13.

The word ‫ܐ‬‫ܬ‬ is written in two strokes: one for ‫ܬ‬ and the other for ‫ܐ‬. Simply follow the points.

Review

- We introduced the last four letters of the alphabet: ‫ܩ‬ (Qoph, close to *q*), ‫ܪ‬ (Rish, rolled *r*), ‫ܫ‬ (Shin, *sh*), and ‫ܬ‬ (Taw, *t*).
- When ‫ܪ‬ is connected to the preceding letter, it takes a different shape as in ‫ܒ݁ܪܐ‬ 'son'. When ‫ܬ‬ connects to the preceding letter, it takes a shape as in ‫ܒ݁ܝܬ݁ܐ‬ 'house'.
- This section covered the following new words:

high	‫ܪܵܡܵܐ‬
big	‫ܪܲܒ݁ܵܐ‬
now	‫ܗܵܫܵܐ‬
sister	‫ܚܵܬ݂ܵܐ‬
Christ	‫ܡܫܝܼܚܵܐ‬
Lord	‫ܡܵܪܝܵܐ‬
spirit	‫ܪܘܿܚܵܐ‬
holy	‫ܩܲܕ݁ܝܼܫܵܐ‬
true	‫ܫܲܪܝܼܪܵܐ‬
said	‫ܐܸܡܲܪ‬
went out	‫ܢܦܲܩ‬
son	‫ܒ݁ܪܐ‬
name	‫ܫܸܡܵܐ‬
house	‫ܒ݁ܝܬ݁ܐ‬

Exercise

1. Put vowels on the following sentences:

a   ‫ܢܦܩ ܒܪܐ ܘܚܬܐ ܡܢ ܡܕܝܢܬܐ‬

b   ‫ܐܡܪ ܡܪܝܐ ܫܡܐ ܪܒܐ ܗܘܐ‬

c   ‫ܪܡܐ ܗܘܐ ܫܡܐ ܩܕܝܫܐ‬

2. Translate the sentences in 1 into English (‫ܡܕܝܼܢܬ݁ܐ‬, with a silent ‫ܬ‬, means *city*).

3. Translate into Syriac:

      a. A good and true uncle went to the city.

      b. Lord God, give me bread (ܠܚܡܐ) and fish of the sea.

      c. Now, this servant ate the nuts, and went to the big house.

8   Review of the Alphabet

Congratulations! You now know the entire Syriac alphabet. Before going forward, let us review the alphabet and learn something new: *Rukokho* and *Qushoyo*.

First, here is a table of the entire alphabet.

Name	Syriac	Sound
Olaph	ܐ	(silent)
Béth	ܒ	b as in *boy*
Gomal	ܓ	g as in *give*
Dolath	ܕ	d as in *dad*
Hé	ܗ	h as in *home*
Waw	ܘ	w as in *we*
Zayn	ܙ	z as in *zebra*
Ḥéth	ܚ	ḥ (listen to the CD)
Ṭéth	ܛ	ṭ (listen to the CD)
Yudh	ܝ	y as in *yet*
Koph	ܟ	k as in *kilo*
Lomadh	ܠ	l as in *let*
Mim	ܡ	m as in *meet*
Nun	ܢ	n as in *not*
Simkath	ܣ	s as in *sand*
ʿé	ܥ	(listen to the CD)
Phe	ܦ	f as in *fat*
Ṣodhé	ܨ	ṣ (listen to the CD)
Qoph	ܩ	q (listen to the CD)
Rish	ܪ	r (rolled)
Shin	ܫ	sh as in *shame*
Taw	ܬ	t as in *tea*

It would be a good thing if you can start remembering the sequence of the letters so that you can look things up in a dictionary. The CD has a song that will help you do that, or you can memorize the mnemonic:

ܐܒܓܕ ܗܘܙ ܚܛܝ ܟܠܡܢ ܣܥܦܨ ܩܪܫܬ

The following table shows the various shapes of letters depending on their position in the word. The names are now given in the Syriac script.

Name	Final Position	Middle Position	Initial Position	Stand-alone Position
ܐܵܠܲܦ	‍ܠ	‍ܠ	ܐ	ܐ
ܒܹܝܬ	‍ܒ	‍ܒ‍	ܒ‍	ܒ
ܓܵܡܲܠ	‍ܓ	‍ܓ‍	ܓ‍	ܓ
ܕܵܠܲܕ	‍ܕ	‍ܕ‍	ܕ‍	ܕ
ܗܹܐ	‍ܗ	‍ܗ‍	ܗ‍	ܗ
ܘܵܘ	‍ܘ	‍ܘ‍	ܘ	ܘ
ܙܲܝܢ	‍ܙ	‍ܙ‍	ܙ	ܙ
ܚܹܝܬ	‍ܚ	‍ܚ‍	ܚ‍	ܚ
ܛܹܝܬ	‍ܛ	‍ܛ‍	ܛ‍	ܛ
ܝܘܼܕ	‍ܝ	‍ܝ‍	ܝ‍	ܝ
ܟܵܦ	‍ܟ	‍ܟ‍	ܟ‍	ܟ
ܠܵܡܲܕ	‍ܠ	‍ܠ‍	ܠ‍	ܠ
ܡܝܼܡ	‍ܡ	‍ܡ‍	ܡ‍	ܡ
ܢܘܼܢ	‍ܢ	‍ܢ‍	ܢ‍	ܢ
ܣܸܡܟܲܬ	‍ܣ	‍ܣ‍	ܣ‍	ܣ
ܥܹܐ	‍ܥ	‍ܥ‍	ܥ‍	ܥ
ܦܹܐ	‍ܦ	‍ܦ‍	ܦ‍	ܦ
ܨܵܕܹܐ	‍ܨ	‍ܨ‍	ܨ‍	ܨ
ܩܘܿܦ	‍ܩ	‍ܩ‍	ܩ‍	ܩ
ܪܹܝܫ	‍ܪ	‍ܪ‍	ܪ	ܪ
ܫܝܼܢ	‍ܫ	‍ܫ‍	ܫ‍	ܫ
ܬܵܘ	‍ܬ	‍ܬ‍	ܬ‍	ܬ

Let us also review the vowels:

Name	Shape	Sound
ܦܬ݂ܵܚܵܐ	◌ܲ	Read *a* as in *man*
ܪܒ݂ܵܨܵܐ	◌ܿ	Read *o* as in *go*
ܙܩܵܦ݂ܵܐ	◌݁	Read *e* as in *men*

ܣܕܪܐ   ⊙̇   Read *ee* as in *meet*

ܚܪܙܐ   ⊙̣   Read *oo* as in *boo*

Rukokho and Qushoyo

If you have paid attention to the readings on the CD, you may have noticed that some letters sound differently in different words, or even in the same word. Did you notice, for example, how ܟܲܝܬܐ 'house' and ܚܵܬܐ 'sister' were pronounced? You may have noticed that while ܬ in ܟܲܝܬܐ sounded like *t* as expected (*bayto*), in ܚܵܬܐ it sounded like *th* in *thin* (*hotho*). In fact, ܬ has those two sounds. Sometimes it is read *t* and sometimes *th* as in *thin*.

Determining if a ܬ should be pronounced *t* or *th* is a complex business, and there is a whole section devoted to the subject in Chapter 7. It turns out that Syriac has a way to indicate the sound. A *t* sound is marked by a little dot on top of the letter as in ܟܲܝܬܐ, while the *th* sound by a little dot under the letter as in ܚܵܬܐ. Now, these dots, like vowel marks, are optional. So far we have not used these dots, but we shall do so from now on.

Another letter that has two sounds is ܟ. The usual sound is *k* as in ܟ̇ܠ 'every', pronounced *kool* or like English *cool*. The other sound does not have a counterpart in English. If you know German, it sounds like *ch* in *acht* 'eight'. If you know Arabic, it sounds like ﺥ. If you know neither, listen to the CD! In Roman letters, we sometimes transliterate this sound as *kh* (not that it sounds like that). Again, Syriac has a way to mark these sounds. A *k* sound is with a dot above the letter as in ܟ̇ܠ 'every', and a *kh* sound is with a dot under the letter as in ܐ̣ܟܠ 'he eats'.

A third letter that has two sounds is ܓ. The usual sound is *g* as in ܓܡܠܐ 'camel'. The other sound also does not exist in English—surprise, surprise! If you know French, it sounds like *r* in *Paris* (as the French say it). If you know Arabic, it sounds like ﻍ. This latter sound is transcribed into Roman letters as *gh* (again, not that it sounds like that). The *g* sound is indicated with a dot above the letter as in ܓ̇ܡܠܐ, while the *gh* sound with a dot under as in ܒ̣ܣܪܐ 'flesh'.

We are not done. There are three more letters to go, but these are less frequently used by Syriac speakers themselves. I shall introduce them, however, for completeness.

The letter ܕ is pronounced as *d* as in ܕܗܒܐ 'gold' with a dot above the letter. The other sound is like *th* in *that*; e.g., ܐ̣ܒܐ with a dot below the letter (so you end up with two dots, the original dot which is larger and the sound indicator dot which is smaller). The ܘ sound is still observed and you will hear it on the CD, but not to the same extent as the ܠ, ܒ or ܓ sounds.

The two remaining sound variations are almost never used today, except by a few pedantic individuals like myself who have nothing better to worry about. The letter ܒ with a dot above sounds like *b* as we already learned. The other variation is ܒ which sounds like *v*. As I said, no one today reads it as *v*. Finally, the letter ܦ sounds like *p*, and no one uses this sound today. The variant sound is ܦ and is the *f* sound we have been using thus far. (The sounds *v* and *p* are used in East Syriac, however, for which see Chapter 8.)

So what are *Rukokho* and *Qushoyo*?

They are exactly what I have just explained. Letters with a dot above are called by Syriac grammarians ܩܘܫܝܐ, *Qushoyo*, meaning a *hard* sound. Letters with a dot below are called ܪܘܟܟܐ, *Rukokho*, meaning a *soft* sound. The six letters which have these sound variations are known by the mnemonic ܒܓܕܟܦܬ.

I don't want to bother you much with these sounds, so let's agree on the following policy. There is no need to put a dot above a letter. If there is no dot, we assume the usual sound: ܒ is *b*, ܓ is *g*, ܕ is *d*, ܟ is *k* and ܬ is *t*—but ܦ is *f*. I shall mark the alternative sound only in words when the alternative sound prevails in contemporary usage; i.e., only for ܓ, ܒ, and ܬ (sometimes ܕ as well).

Here are the words we learned in this chapter for which we should start applying soft sounds. Remember, we will only mark soft sounds with a dot below: ܐܝܕܐ 'hand', ܐܟܠ 'ate', ܒܓܕܐܕ 'Baghdad', ܓܘ 'inside', ܗܕܐ 'this (f.)', ܚܕ 'one (m.)', ܚܕܐ 'one (f.)', ܚܬܐ 'sister', and ܡܕܝܢܬܐ 'city'.

9   I Don't Need Those Vowels, Do I?

So far we have been reading 'vocalized' Syriac. That is, the vowel marks were fully written on each word. In reality, Syriac is usually written without vowel marks considering that vowel marks did not even appear until the seventh century. This is actually not as bad as it sounds as you will see below. The ancients did it, so can you!

Let us start by reading some English sentences. Can you read the following?

1. *I slept on the bd.*
2. *I ate a hmbrgr.*
3. *pls brng me a book.*
4. *I wnt to school*
5. *I wnt to eat.*

You probably figured out that *bd* in sentence 1 is *bed* but without the *e*, and *hmbrgr* in sentence 2 is *hamburger* without the vowels. Similarly, the first two words in sentence 3 are *please bring*. See it is not that bad after all.

How did you read *wnt* in sentences 4 and 5? If you got it right, you would have read *went* in sentence 4. Actually, in sentence 5 it can be read either as *want* or *went*. This is an example of how a word written without vowels can be read in two (sometimes more) different ways. In most cases, as in sentence 4, the context of the sentence makes it clear as to which word you should be reading. In some cases, as in sentence 5, the sentence is not enough and one needs a larger context.

Syriac operates in this same fashion. When you learn new words, try to learn them with and without the vowels.

I promise to take it easy on you. Let us start omitting vowels one step at a time.

Do I Really Need ?

You may have noticed that the vast majority of nouns end in ܐ such as ܐܰܒܐ 'father,' ܐܶܡܐ 'mother,' and ܗܰܒܒܐ 'flower'. Since we know that the last vowel is , let us take it out. For example, the previous three words can be written ܐܰܒ, ܐܶܡ and ܗܰܒܒ. Here are more words:

high	ro-mo	ܪܳܡܐ	1
big	ra-bo	ܪܰܒܐ	2
now	ho-sho	ܗܳܫܐ	3
sister	ḥo-tho	ܚܳܬܐ	4
Christ	m-shi-ḥo	ܡܫܺܝܚܐ	5
Lord	mor-yo	ܡܳܪܝܐ	6
spirit	roo-ḥo	ܪܽܘܚܐ	7
holy	qa-dee-sho	ܩܰܕܺܝܫܐ	8
true	sha-ree-eo	ܫܰܪܺܝܪܐ	9

Let us review some phrases from the previous section, but now we will omit the final ܳ.

1 ܫܡܥܐ ܘܐܕܐ ܘܘܚܕܐ

2 ܘܪܘܚܐ ܩܕܝܫܐ ܡܢ ܐܠܗܐ ܫܪܝܪܐ

3 ܡܪܝܐ ܐܠܗܐ

4 ܡܫܝܚܐ ܕܐ ܘܐܠܗܐ ܐܕܐ

5 ܫܠܡܐ ܘܐܕܐ ܘܪܡܐ

When Can I Omit ܳ?

We studied before (see section 1.6) that plurals of masculine nouns tend to end in ܶܐ rather than ܳܐ. Additionally, the plurals take the two-dot *syomé* as in ܢܳܡܘܣܶܐ 'laws'. In such cases, we can omit the ܳ vowel as the two-dot *syomé* is a sufficient indicator. Hence, we can write ܢܳܡܘܣܐ 'law' (read *no-moo-so*), and ܢܳܡܘܣܶܐ 'laws' (read *no-moo-sé*).

Here are additional examples for practice:

world	ʿol-mo	ܥܳܠܡܐ	1
worlds	ʿol-mé	ܥܳܠܡܶܐ	2
people	ʿa-mo	ܥܰܡܐ	3

peoples	ʿa-mé	ܥܰܡ̈ܶܐ	4
slave	ʿab-do	ܥܰܒܕܳܐ	5
slaves	ʿab-dé	ܥܰܒܕ̈ܶܐ	6

How about Doing Without ◌ܽ?

Recall that when we introduced ◌ܽ we also said that it is always followed by ܘ as in ܢܳܡܽܘܣܳܐ 'law,' ܢܽܘܢܳܐ 'fish', etc. In fact, it is the combination ܘ◌ܽ that makes this vowel.

This does not mean that the reverse is true. If there is a ܘ in a word, it may be preceded by ◌ܰ as in ܨܰܘܡܳܐ 'fast.'

So let's make a deal. When we have ܘ◌ܽ in a word, we will omit the ◌ܽ. The ܘ is enough to tell us that the vowel is there. For example, we will say ܢܘܢܐ for ܢܽܘܢܳܐ and ܢܳܡܘܣܐ for ܢܳܡܽܘܣܳܐ. (Remember, we are omitting the final ◌ܳ as well.) But we will keep showing ◌ܰ as in ܨܰܘܡܐ for ܨܰܘܡܳܐ 'fast'.

Let us practice reading some words:

spirit	roo-ḥo	ܪܘܚܐ	1
law	no-moo-so	ܢܳܡܘܣܐ	2
fish	noo-no	ܢܘܢܐ	3

Can I Omit ◌ܺ Now?

OK, we are getting there. So far we were able to omit ◌ܳ at the end of words, and ◌ܽ because it is usually followed by ܘ. Now, we will try to omit ◌ܺ in a specific context.

You may have noticed that ◌ܺ is usually followed by ܝ as in ܪܺܝܫܐ 'head'. (Again, the opposite does not hold as ܝ can be preceded by ◌ܰ or ◌ܳ as in ܒܰܝܬܐ 'house' and ܩܳܝܡܐ 'she rises'.) So whenever we have the combination ܝ◌ܺ, we will omit the vowel as in ܪܝܫܐ 'head' for ܪܺܝܫܐ, and ܐܝܕܐ 'hand' for ܐܺܝܕܐ. But we will show other vowels before ܝ as in ܒܰܝܬܐ 'house' for ܒܰܝܬܳܐ.

Here are some words for practice:

hand	ee-do	ܐܝܕܐ	1
which (f.)	ay-do	ܐܰܝܕܐ	2
true	sha-ree-ro	ܫܰܪܝܪܐ	3

Review

- Syriac is usually written without vowel marks. We will begin omitting vowels bit by bit.

- When a word ends in ܐܳ, we will not show the ܳ as in ܐܒ for ܐܰܒܳ 'father'.

- When a masculine plural word ends in ܐܳ, we will not show the ܳ as in ܢܩ̈ܐ for ܢܩ̈ܐ. The two-dot *syomé* indicates that the word is plural.

- When ܘ is preceded by ܳ in the combination ܘܳ, we will omit the vowel mark as ܒܘܡܐ for ܒܽܘܡܳ 'owl', but we will keep other vowels before ܘ as in ܝܘܡܐ 'day' for ܝܰܘܡܳ.

- When ܝ is preceded by ܳ in the combination ܝܳ, we will omit the vowel mark as ܐܝܕܐ for ܐܺܝܕܳ 'hand', but we will keep other vowels before ܝ as in ܒܝܬܐ 'house' for ܒܰܝܬܳ.